Woman of Faith

An Inspirational Book

By

SKYYE HOWZE

Copyright © 2020 by Skyye Howze
All rights reserved

No part of this book may be reproduced, stored in or introduced into a retrieval system, or transmitted, in any form or by any means (electronic, mechanical, photocopying, recording, or otherwise) without prior written permission from the publisher.

ISBN: 9798686334557

The scriptures in this book are quoted from the New International Version (NIV) Holy Bible, New International Version®, NIV® Copyright ©1973, 1978, 1984, 2011 by Biblica, Inc.® Used by permission. All rights reserved worldwide,

For information on the content of this book, email skyyehowze@yahoo.com

WrightStuf Consulting, LLC
Columbia, SC
www.wrightstuf.com

Printed in the United States of America

Introduction

Now Faith is the substance of things hoped for but the evidence of not being seen (Hebrew 11). Merely, if we must walk by faith and not by sight, do we lose our way from all the craziness we face? Absolutely, but God wants you to become a woman of faith and to allow whatever it is that is trying to downsize your faith to cut loose and keep believing that God can fix it, change it. But only when you operate in faith as the woman you are. We determine how we use our faith, so be mindful of how you touch God with it. He is the position to blow your mind in every area with the help and support of your faith. I encourage you to get started filling your mind, heart, mind, and soul with faith so God can give you a head start on all he has for you merely as a woman who is searching for bigger faith.

Life's Struggles

The struggles of life try to break us all. We lose faith along the way. We are sometimes unsure which way to go because we're stagnant in the very thing that's trying to take us out. While we are stuck, we don't see how we can come out. The ups and downs blindside us. It allows us to see confusion, keep us bound, and going in the wrong direction when we knew that all we had to do was to come to God. Instead, we do it our way, which makes the struggle harder. Your faith counts. Use it to get the better life you need.

Meditate on this scripture: Psalm 23:4

Even though I walk

through the darkest valley,

I will fear no evil,

for you are with me;

your rod and your staff,

they comfort me.

Pray this Prayer

Dear Heavenly Father,

You know what we face, and it isn't always easy. Keep us in troubled times when we feel like giving up. Give us the strength to push forward. Your joy is needed in this very hour. Our lives depend on it. We will make it farther just because of who you are and what you stand for. In Jesus's name, Amen.

Your thoughts & prayer

Obedience

Obedience is better than sacrifice. God requires us to be obedient in our toughest season and everyday life. Although we don't understand, we can be assured that God will reward what he asked you to do. Never rebel against obedience. He will test you in that same area to show you who you are in him, and to see if you trust what he speaks. When he says obey, please don't go astray. Please listen as he speaks to your heart to make that ultimate sacrifice of being obedient.

Meditate on this scripture: Deuteronomy 5:33

Walk in obedience to all that the LORD your God has commanded you, so that you may live and prosper and prolong your days in the land that you will possess.

Pray this Prayer

Dear God,

You are the way. Without your commandments, it's impossible to live. We would find ourselves lost as we face today. Also, help us to live out of obedience. Obeying you is what counts even when it doesn't make an ounce of sense to us. Let us be sensitive to your spirit, slow to speak, but quick to hear your voice to listen for the instructions of obedience. In Jesus's name, Amen.☺

Your thoughts & prayer

Death

 When death arrives, you grieve with no time limit. You are sure that you will heal but don't know when, so you crumble more in secrets, not moving forward, and allowing death to take over your mind. Death is painful, and it's hard to receive. No one knows when they will exit this world. Only God knows. Sometimes we prepare for our own funerals on earth - spiritual death that is, which keeps you going around in circles and doubting what God can do. Death is not the answer, nor is it the first thing to consider, but it's a very real place for us all.

Meditate on this scripture: *Romans 8:38-39*

For I am convinced that neither death nor life, neither angels nor demons,[a] neither the present nor the future, nor any powers, 39 neither height nor depth, nor anything else in all creation, will be able to separate us from the love of God that is in Christ Jesus our Lord.

Pray this Prayer

Dear Living God,

Death is challenging, naturally and spiritually. When we die, we cringe to live like you, but in order to receive life on your belief, we have to experience death in the midst of the dying. Let us survive in case someone wants to embalm us alive. We want to arise in your power from the dirt of death. Help us find our way with the shovel of your grace. In Jesus's name, Amen. ☺

Your thoughts & prayer

Holy Spirit

 The Holy Spirit is a refreshing wind that allows your soul to breathe a second wind. If you haven't experienced the overwhelming feeling of God's presence of aroma all over your body, you are truly missing out on how he can take you on a high that's unthinkable while your mind, body, and soul alarm loud from hurt. The Holy Spirit to minister to the areas you are broken and lacking in for you will see a shift in your life as the Holy Spirit take over all the hurts that are deep-rooted.

Meditate on this scripture: Titus 3:5, 6

He saved us, not because of righteous things we had done, but because of his mercy. He saved us through the washing of rebirth and renewal by the Holy Spirit, whom he poured out on us generously through Jesus Christ our Savior.

Pray this Prayer

Dear Almighty One,

Fall fresh on us. Show us and help wherever we are weak, for we don't know the outcome. Give us words that we can't express on our own. Allow your presence to show in such a way that it grabs everyone's attention from restraining to restoration. In Jesus's name. Amen.

Your thoughts & prayer

Authority

God gives us all the authority to rule and reign in his name. Do you know the power you have to change lives and to cast out demons, making them flee from you and your family? The authority you have is for the nations. God gave it to you. Stand tall and show the world how God shines through you with power and Authority.

Meditate on this scripture: Luke 9:1

When Jesus had called the Twelve together, he gave them power and authority to drive out all demons and to cure diseases.

Pray this Prayer

Dear Yahweh,

Help us to understand that your submission is vital for the authority you have placed on our lives and given us to carry.

You gave us free will to live in your power under our calling and the knowledge to use it wisely. We know who you are and what you stand for in our lives, but don't let us lean to our own understanding but be directed through you to run with authority. In Jesus's name. Amen.

Your thoughts & prayer

Salvation

Don't mind what people say about your salvation. Pick salvation over the naysayers, the judgmental, the perfect ones, and the jealous ones. God needs you to have salvation, not just for you but for the world. If you dismiss what he's doing through you, you will fall or even be like Judas and betray him. Salvation is the call to shift you from being a sinner and to be transformed into a saint. Which will you choose today? I say, choose salvation.

Meditate on this scripture: Romans 10:9-10

If you declare with your mouth, "Jesus is Lord," and believe in your heart that God raised him from the dead, you will be saved. For it is with your heart that you believe and are justified, and it is with your mouth that you profess your faith and are saved.

Pray this Prayer

Dear Heavenly Father,

Help us understand that salvation is professed with an unreal sign of faith for us all to believe and have the confidence to say life is worth living. In our trials, let us be the one used for your glory no matter who tries to destroy us, who walk away, or have the potential to stay. Let us gain a heart and stand boldly for Christ, have that zeal to thrust for righteousness, and thrust for salvation. Amen.

Your thoughts & prayer

Trust

Trusting can be a difficult thing to do with people and even sometimes with God. Still, in this hour, God wants to know do you trust him not for material things but for his promise and purpose that needs to be birth through your life. Often, we try to make life a place where we cope with our pain without God's power today trust (T)ake (R)esponsiblity for the (U)nseen (S)tages of (T)riumph.

Meditate on this scripture: Psalm 20:7

Some trust in chariots and some in horses, but we trust in the name of the Lord our God.

Pray this Prayer

Dear God,

When we are afraid, help us to trust more. You can keep all of our secrets because you know us best. That's why we vent to you. Help us stay safe so we can always thrive like a green leaf overflowing with joy and peace to trust you. Amen.

Your thoughts & prayer

Waiting

Waiting for his word is sometimes hard? Do you have a problem with waiting? Or do you question why God is taking so long? I'll be the first to answer. WE AREN'T READY!! However, continue to wait on the Lord, for he knows where we are going and how we are getting there. We don't want to rush the promise; we want to prepare for the promise. Don't be in a hurry; be patient in your waiting. Your reward is in your sacrifice, suffering, and stillness.

Meditate on this scripture: *Micah 7:7*

But as for me, I watch in hope for the Lord, I wait for God my Savior; my God will hear me.

Pray this Prayer

Dear, Living God,

Help us to wait for the promise. When we get antsy, calm our spirits of anxiousness or any form of anxiety. Lord, build our nervous systems to align properly with your word coming subjected to your voice as you speak. God, you know the beginning and the end. Let our hearts take courage in simply waiting on you, In Jesus's name. Amen.

Your thoughts & prayer

Loneliness

When loneliness occurs, the bell of boredom rings. It's a sign to inform you just how lonely you are. Being lonely can deceive you into doing the wrong things. Your flesh starts to crave for the ungodly things while loneliness alarm loud in your heart. You fall into the trap of sin. Sometimes we have to suffer in loneliness because we have been elevated in God, or we have an assignment that causes us to disappear into isolation. But this bad feeling sometimes makes us feel unworthy. Still, the key thing to all of this is to stay pure in your time of loneliness.

Meditate on this scripture: Proverbs 18:24

One who has unreliable friends soon comes to ruin, but there is a friend who sticks closer than a brother.

Pray this Prayer

Dear Sovereign One,

I may have slipped up. I may have done wrong, but as I continue on a clean slate to purity, help me to cope with my loneliness. Help me to see things the way you see them, help me to be okay knowing that even while being lonely, I'm not alone and will always have you. Amen.

Your thoughts & prayer

Just

(J)ump and (U)nderstand the (S)avior's (T)imetable. Being just is the ultimate goal to follow God wholeheartedly. He shows us how to stay in his time rather than moving from our own timetable when we think we have it figured out. We don't allow ourselves to speak, saying the just shall live by faith. We can't do anything without the father. Be "Just" in this hour, for when you do, God will give you your heart's desire for not only obeying, but simply being JUST!!

Meditate on this scripture: Hebrews 4:16

Let us then approach God's throne of grace with confidence, so that we may receive mercy and find grace to help us in our time of need.

Pray this Prayer

Dear Father,

While many are being jealous, help them to be just, help them to flow with how you move. The time will come where we will have to decide to be just. Give us clarification in our thinking. We want to do the right thing concerning your will and time. Help us to do the right thing so we won't suffer in the long run from doing the wrong thing. Amen.

Your thoughts & prayer

Forgave

 I forgave you!! That's what I said to the person who had me numb in pain, but in reality, I didn't. My heart spoke evil instead of "I forgive. At some point in our lives, we have said I forgave him/her, and the heart doesn't match up with the words. Out of the heart flows the issues of life. Did you know? God forgave on all occasions. He knew the true meaning behind it while we, as people, hold on to so much. God is in the position to tell you, *No, let it go, I forgave you, so you have to forgive others.* Don't walk around grooved with bitterness in your heart. Be FREE today to forgive so others can say with sincerity, "Someone truly forgave me."

Meditate on this scripture: Ephesians 4:32
Be kind and compassionate to one another, forgiving each other, just as in Christ God forgave you.

Pray this Prayer

Dear God,

The joy of forgiveness is the epitome of your glory. Sure we want to do things our way but help us to see that you are the only way; the forgiven way. We want to glean from your life as you are an example to us, the dark world, the sinners, and the saints. You went through a lot to get us where we need to be in life. Just as salvation is free, let our hearts be as free as it needs to be to forgive the ones who hurt us. In Jesus's name. Amen.

Your thoughts & prayer

Love

Love yourself with God's Love. Our love can sometimes be weak and perhaps immature, especially when it's being tried. I never knew how to love until I came to Christ. I wasn't brought up in love. I wasn't shown, love. I was neglected and abandoned. The love I thought I was receiving was survival mode to help me cope through my life of trauma. God's love is the love to run to, not from. You won't find it in a man, through sex, or any form of relationship that is willing to express love differently than God. Take it from me. It can be pretty but false. Love on God's level. It will help you, not only love yourself but your enemies too!

Meditate on this scripture: 1 Corinthians 16:14
Do everything in love.

Pray this Prayer

Dear Heavenly Father,

Give us the faith to trust your love over human love, for we know we can get so wrapped up in false love, it will blind spiritually. We want to grow more with how to love like you. The process can be daunting sometimes, but the reward will be worth it. As we go through this life, give us the strength to love, love, love, and love out loud. Amen.

Your thoughts & prayer

Memory

The real-life memory I have carried has caused me to lose the memory of who God was and is in my life. As my soul was tied to a fairytale, I choose the fairytale over God, and it caused a major memory loss to the things of God and who I was in him. You may have a memory you are wrapping yourself up in, struggling to find your way. The memory is feeling good, but it fades. Let it go and hold on to the memory of God, for his memory is everlasting. It's something you can grasp and take in when everything around you is vaporizing. You will be in a place of receiving all he has for you in majestic ways.

Meditate on this scripture: 2 Timothy 1:7

For the Spirit God gave us does not make us timid, but gives us power, love and self-discipline.

Pray this Prayer

Dear Living God,

Whatever memory we can't seem to let go of and is not to your liking, free us from it. Help us to be free from it, so we can feel the real memory of knowing who you are personally. Give us the strength to hold on to you until the imaginary memory fades. Only you can fix the loss, making it a gain so we can fully operate in you.

Your thoughts & prayer

Zoned

 I am zoned to the ungodly things, and I can't seem to be visual to the tragic scenes. God gave me extra senses to keep the tactics from the enemy away. Zone from the things that caused me to sin. I am zoned from the time of shame. I am zoned for the wars in the nations, zoned from the hectic things that are trying to destroy my mental. I am zoned from the burdens I carried. I am zoned from the rejection that trust to cover my heart in the blindness of hurt. You don't have to be zoned out in this hour. Oh, never mind!! It's vital to protect everything you can. Zone out to the world but be zoned and willing to God. There's no force but the extra push to keep you from being zoned.

Meditate on this scripture: Acts 20:28

Keep watch over yourselves and all the flock of which the Holy Spirit has made you overseers. Be shepherds of the church of God, which he bought with his own blood.

Pray this Prayer

Dear Father of the Most High,

Help me to be zoned out to the things that are trying to take my focus off you. We know that if we are zoned into you, we can not only cast our cares but see the zone shift from adversity to ascending peace. Keep us alert, keep us wise, keep us alive. In Jesus's mighty name. Amen.

Your thoughts & prayer

Unashamed

If I am ashamed, then that means I can't be unashamed. While many pretend to love you, I actually love you for dying for me. I stand up for you. Young, saved, and truly unashamed. I boldly gave my life to Christ, and you pulled me and set me apart from a dying world. You even allowed me to go back in it but only to show me that you can still anchor me and pulled me from the snares of the enemy. OH MY!! How awesome is that? I am unapologetically unashamed and in a place of seeking all you have for me.

For you, the reader, never be ashamed of the Sovereign One. He brought me out of the trenches when I almost lost my mind. He suddenly freed me, and now I walk in victory unashamed, and you will soon do the same ;).

Meditate on this scripture: 1 John 2:28

And now, dear children, continue in him, so that when he appears we may be confident and unashamed before him at his coming.

Pray this Prayer

Dear YAHWEH,

You have given me (us) the answer on the cross, longing for your touch when all we did was receive your blood. It saved us. It caused us to live and not be ashamed. In this season, we walk unashamed. Give us the mercy and grace to say to the dying world that we no longer fear what man has to say. We don't walk in shame; we boldly confess in your son, Jesus's name. Amen.

Your thoughts & prayer

Pulling Together

There is a time and a season for everything (Ecclesiastes 3:1). You have to know that we are not on earth to be alone. Pull together, husband and wife, pull together mother and daughter, pull together father and son, pull together family members and church members. The signs of end times are not to isolate you but the pulling together in desperation for a cry of help. A cry for healing, a cry for deliverance, a cry for the things of God. Pulling together is the joy of God's glory and for others to see his manifestation. You must be in the position to fight through the odds of life. Time waits on no one. Don't allow people and things rob you from pulling together. You have the favor to pull together and show God that you are worthy in his eyesight to please only him and not people.

Meditate on this scripture: Numbers 1:18

...and they called the whole community together on the first day of the second month. The people registered their ancestry by their clans and families, and the men twenty years old or more were listed by name, one by one...

Pray this Prayer

Dear God,

You have what we need to mend the broken pieces. You have what we need to repair marriages. You also have the cure to the diseases we carry, such as heartbreaks, wounds, scars, and tenders spots that make us ache in unfavorable ways. You are in control of our life. Be the glue to pull us together. Amen.

Your thoughts & prayer

Revealed

The signs of healing we need to reveal can be revealed through you. You told us that you are Rafa. Keep showing us the hidden things of you, the next dimension of life, the time of structure to catapult us into the unseen. You revealed and will keep revealing bountifully. You said that whatever we asked for, we could have. We need you to reveal all your good secrets of MIRACLE, SIGNS, AND WONDERS! You can reveal. We want to tell and show the world how real you are in our lives. If you reveal who we really are, it would be the true identity of Christ. We need you to keep us alive in your revealing. Allow your light to shine on people so it can reach their darkness, and even ourselves. Revealing can help us grow in our weak areas and sometimes be hard to receive but allow us to say, "Ouch," and keep it moving to whatever you revealed and will be revealing.

Meditate on this scripture: Genesis 35:7

There he built an altar, and he called the place El Bethel, because it was there that God revealed himself to him when he was fleeing from his brother.

Pray this Prayer

Dear Heavenly Father,

Keep the lens on our eyes. Uncover as you reveal the truths, the ugly ones, for we know what it's like to be revealed. Give us the ears to hear as well as our soul to grasp all that you revealed. Life is like a vapor, but don't allow us to fade away before the revealing of your coming. Keep us prepared. In Jesus's mighty name. Amen.

Your thoughts & prayer

Wonders

The wonders we long to see are the healing in broken people. You show up in powerful ways, ministering to the cracked souls and damaged spirits like a rushing wind. You take every part of our bodies and restrict every broken bone, blowing fresh wind that causes a fresh fire to ignite us to be the wonder the world needs. The wonders we long for is the epitome of deliverance from being an addict to a substance, sex, any habit you can clean it away. The wonders of what we long to see are the victory of freedom and wholeness to be complete in Christ, in life, and our families. We can seal the bondage, the disposition, the dysfunction with your glory of wonders.

Meditate on this scripture: Deuteronomy 7:19

You saw with your own eyes the great trials, the signs and wonders, the mighty hand and outstretched arm, with which the Lord your God brought you out. The Lord, your God, will do the same to all the peoples you now fear.

Pray this Prayer

Dear Living Father,

Your wonders are the answer to an unbeliever. Allow them to see the miracles. Move your hand in my life and others as well. We want our heart to feel the signs you have created for the earth realm. Make our souls shake and make our spirits so free as if one is floating in it. Show us that wonders can be performed right on earth. In Jesus's name. Amen.

Your thoughts & prayer

Home

Come home. You have wasted life enough; there's no room for slack. Come home; God is waiting. He has the door unlocked for you. Come home. Life is the joy of knowing you have arms to fall in at home. Heaven is orchestrating miracles every day. Home is where the heart is? NO! Home is where God is!! Allow him to sweep you into a room filled with his awesome furniture of favor, comfort, rest, and a "for sure" sign to be placed by the right hand of the father. Come home now. You will never lack. You will never cry again. You will never fold. You are protected at home.

Meditate on this scripture: Exodus 18:23
If you do this and God so commands, you will be able to stand the strain, and all these people will go home satisfied."

Pray this Prayer

Dear Spirit of the Living God,

You promised us a home to stay, to be safe to come, so we don't have to worry. You told us that it is easy for us to step out from home but hard to come back home to the Master. Give us the strength to do the right thing. You can say, and you can do what you please because you are over the whole universe. Continue to ask us to come home. Amen.

Your thoughts & prayer

Demonstration

Be the demonstration everyone can glean from, as you set the example to be fully like Jesus. Show and tell the traits at home and give people your light to shine through their darkness. While many may see you as being like Jesus, through you, all of them can fully embark on the demonstration for the world, for the family, for anyone who lacks Jesus. You can be the light that helps others come out so they can be a light to the world. I'm a demonstration to you as I write I'm ministering to your broken soul to repair and rebuild the brokenness leading you on the right path to Christ while I do this for you, take the lead and pass the torch and be a demonstration too ☺

Meditate on this scripture: Proverbs 16:2

All a person's ways seem pure to them, but motives are weighed by the Lord.

Pray this Prayer

Dear YAHWEH,

Help us to be a demonstration for the broken world, to the people who are blind to you, who wants to see you but don't know how to seek you. All they see is material things, and you are more than that and have way more to offer. You said you would give us perfect peace even in a storm. Be that demonstration today, so we can continue to be one for the people who need you to show us who you are so we can show the world who we can be through you. Amen

Your thoughts & prayer

Extol

God, we extol you because of who you are and what you carry. God, we extol you for the times we wanted to give up. You showed us that as long as we extol you in everything, greatness shall be upon us. God, we extol you for the fruits of multiplicity that the sacrifice sower keeps everything you have given but supersedes into an overflow of more than enough. God, without extolling you, how shall we prosper in health, wealth, knowledge, and wisdom. How shall we prosper from poverty mindsets? How shall we live? How shall we breathe? Let us humbly extol you in all we do.

Meditate on this scripture: Psalm 68:4

Sing to God, sing in praise of his name, extol him who rides on the clouds; rejoice before him — his name is the Lord.

Pray this Prayer

Dear Heavenly Father,

You are worthy to extol. From the rising of the sun, you are the same forever and always. We were created to extol you in difficulties, happiness, love, loneliness, sorrow, and mishaps. We can't make it without you, God. Allow us to live on earth to extol before man. Breathe a fresh wind on us, so we can praise and worship you as you see fit. In Jesus's name. Amen!

Your thoughts & prayer

Alive

 How can you be alive if you are suffocating from the very thing that killed you spiritually or tried to cause death in every area of your life? For you can say I'm alive, but dead on the inside. Life is about getting a hold to God's oxygen to breathe aloud and properly with purity. You want to be alive, but how can you be alive when you are buried with guilt, shame, loss, rejection, addictions, and negativity floating around you. It is designed to suck the life out of you. Premature death is what it is really called. Who are you? Do you know you are under that rock? Come from under there hiding—your life matters. You have a purpose, a very specific reason to live, and a destiny to fulfill. "ARISE AND LIVE." He chooses you to be alive now!

Meditate on this scripture: 1 Samuel 2:6

The Lord brings death and makes alive; he brings down to the grave and raises up.

Pray this Prayer

Dear Living God of the Whole World,

Help keep us alive in this cruel world. Often, we seek to be alive through others and how they see us. You have been the air we need to breathe since you created us. Help us be a living vessel that surrounds others to stay alive as you keep us alive to be used in this hour. Amen.

Your thoughts & prayer

Hindrance

The door of sin crept open in my life when I was in right standards with God. A strong hindrance assured me that life was worth living out of the flesh. As I allowed it to make my decisions, it led me to believe that I was doing right. I got sidetracked as I slipped and dipped into the doorway of a variety of sins. The hindrance caused my body to get attached to a feeling that I never encountered before, one that I craved and longed for. The hindrance became stronger and stronger. It almost had a grip until God spoke to me, saying NO! You can't afford to slip up anymore.

If you do, you will be in a pool of blood, swimming, drowning, and sinking, shipwrecking back into who you used to be. The hindrance almost took me there, but I hid in God a little deeper. He not only spared mc but gave me the grace to make it out of the dangerous game I was playing.

Meditate on this scripture: 1 John 2:2

He is the atoning sacrifice for our sins, and not only for ours but also for the sins of the whole world.

Pray this Prayer

Dear Father of the Most High,

We come against every distraction and hindrance that's trying to knock us off course to do your work for the kingdom. Life can be very tricky if it's not discerned carefully with the things people do. Keep our eyes open to the wolf in sheep's clothing, to the snakes, the leeches, and anything that's trying to rob us of our assignment. We trust that you will give us the wisdom to be wise, watchful, and pray continually on the ones who try to prey on the saints. In your son Jesus's name. Amen.

Your thoughts & prayer

Repentance

 If you want a supernatural encounter, you must have a heart of repentance. In some ways, I felt that I couldn't repent because I simply chose revenge inside. I allowed so much unforgiveness and bitterness, hatred, anger, and pride to rule my life. And because of that, it kept my freedom locked in. Everyone doesn't normally deal with the same struggles. We all do things differently and handle our situations accordingly, but it all is still sin. I became the woman of repentance when I discovered abuse of all forms, along with bad habits and addictions. I gained the heart of repentance when the hurt showed me that life could wipe me out, or I can just keep living. I chose to live as I repented to God, and he restored me bountifully.

Meditate on this scripture: Corinthians 7:10

Make room for us in your hearts. We have wronged no one, we have corrupted no one, we have exploited no one.

Pray this Prayer

Dear Sovereign One,

We all have encountered some sort of abuse, or we may have even been the abuser, but we as a repentance heart, come to you to repent for any wrongdoing we may have caused or anything that has disappointed you. Life can be so routine, and we flow wherever the chips may fall, but, in this hour, we want to stop having a pity party, we want to stop playing the victim and want to be real with you right now! Things in our lives try to break us down, but if we have the boldness to say I repent of all my sins, we can defeat that very thing that is trying to keep us doing wrong. Amen.

Your thoughts & prayer

Conclusion

I hope this book helps you discover the real you as you dig deep down in your thoughts and inner self to see who you are. When you reach up and arise, you will pull out the WOMAN OF FAITH! The woman who has mastered it, the woman who has overcome, the woman who has grown from the caterpillar forming into a beautiful butterfly, to the woman who is ready to SOAR to the next dimension of life.

I pray these writings not only draw you closer to the Almighty One (God), but I also pray it helps to inspire you, uplift you, and allow you to get in touch with your healing. Many blessings to the readers of this book. I hope my words stir the fire in you to keep going even when you don't see your way through. Faith has the outlook to believe still because only God can do the unthinkable. ☺

Read other books by the author. You can find these titles on Amazon.com and other online bookstores.

A Broken That's Unspoken

Gaining Intimacy with God

Dare to Seek

When God Whispers

Longing for God

Touches of Hope

Venting to Heal (with Gwendolyn C. Lewis Johnson)

Crowned Butterfly

Living Right Isn't an Option (It's Mandatory)

Woman of Faith

Tame Your Mental

CRAWL